So Young, So Sad, So Listen

By PHILIP GRAHAM AND CAROL HUGHES
Drawings by Christine Roche

So Young, So Sad, So Listen

GASKELL/WEST LONDON HEALTH PROMOTION AGENCY

Text © The Royal College of Psychiatrists 1995
Drawings © Christine Roche 1995

Gaskell is an imprint of the Royal College of Psychiatrists,
17 Belgrave Square, London SW1X 8PG

British Library Cataloguing-in-Publication Data
Graham, Philip
  So Young, So Sad, So Listen
  I. Title II. Hughes, Carol III. Roche, Christine
  618.928527

ISBN 0-902241-80-X

Distributed in North America
by American Psychiatric Press, Inc.
ISBN 0-88048-641-4

Printed in Great Britain by Bell & Bain Ltd., Glasgow

Contents

Preface   vii

   Introduction   1
1 What is depression?   5
2 Signs of depression   7
3 How common is depression in children and young people?   19
4 What causes depression in children and young people?   22
5 Helping the depressed child — what you (parents, teachers, other children) can do   31
6 The child and family clinic   39
7 What happens to depressed children and young people?   50

   Further reading   51
   Notes on the authors   52
   Note on Defeat Depression Campaign   53
   Helpful addresses   54
   Index   55

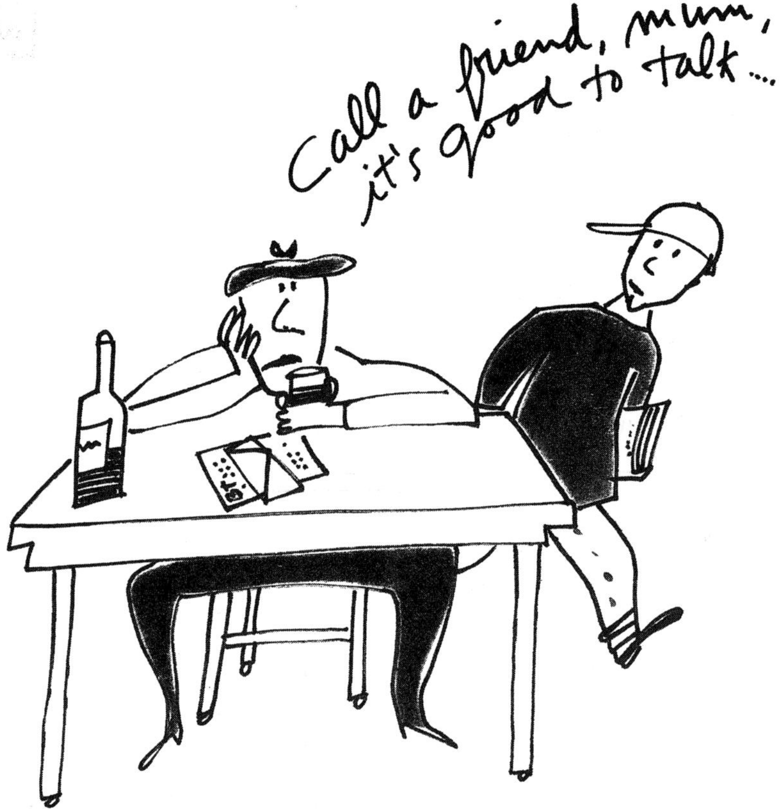
Call a friend, mum, it's good to talk....

Preface

There is hardly a more misunderstood disorder than depression. This at first sight appears paradoxical. After all, the great majority of us from time to time feel low, dispirited and blue. We wonder what the point of life is, and whether we can get it all together to keep going. We all get depressed. And because we do get depressed for short periods and in the face of recognisable difficulties — work stress, marital difficulties, financial pressures, personal diappointments — we conclude that this is what depression means and that it does not amount to very much.

But this is not what depression is, or more accurately, not what clinical depression is. The ordinary day-to-day ebbs and flows of mood are no more than hints of the monstrous storm, what novelist and sufferer William Styron has termed "a veritable howling tempest in the brain", which is depressive illness. Public and personal ignorance of depression contribute significantly to the situation wherein many people still suffer needlessly and agonisingly, and all too many more in deep despair take their own lives. Still too many of us unthinkingly exhort seriously depressed people to pull themselves together and look on the bright side, unaware of or ignoring the reality that, were the depressed able to do such a thing, they would not remain depressed in the first place.

If many people have difficulty understanding depression and empathising with the depressed, even more find it exceedingly difficult to understand that children can get profoundly depressed too. This is partly due to the persistence of the belief in the innocence of childhood and the notion of depression as an adult reaction to the strains and stresses of mature life. Yet it is not as if there is a lack of evidence concerning the vicissitudes of early life. Childhood bereavement is a case in point. C. S. Lewis, writing of his mother's death, observed that with it "all that was tranquil and reliable disappeared from my life". J. M. Barrie never recovered from the psychological impact on him of his mother's pathological grieving on the death of his older brother, her eldest son. Many children, with love, support and understanding, survive and grow through bereavement and other losses. Many, however, experience serious and disabling depression requiring intervention and help. Consider too those more terrible experiences of which we are becoming increasingly aware — children exposed to persistent sexual abuse, to the vagaries, violence and unpredictabilities of life with a substance-abusing parent, to the bitterness, manipulations and destructiveness of severe marital disharmony, to the corrosive toll of chronic, disabling physical disease. Undetected, unsupported, untreated, many such children grow up to live seriously blighted and impoverished adult lives.

This book takes seriously the phenomenon of childhood depression, but it is not alarmist. Rather, it dispels ignorance and provides information in a calm and rational way to help all of us — parents, other family members, teachers, doctors, social workers — who find ourselves in positions which bring us into contact with children in pain, difficulty and despair.

Professor Anthony Clare

Introduction

This book is about depression in children and teenagers during their school years, from 5 to 16. It is written for parents and teachers. We also hope that social workers, health visitors and family doctors will find it useful. Perhaps some teenagers themselves might find it interesting.

Do children and young teenagers really get depressed? Here are three accounts of depression about three different children, described by a mother, a teacher, and a 14-year-old girl herself. (The names and some details have been changed.)

The mother

Ben's mother, an art teacher, describes the change that came over him after a short viral illness.

"He changed somehow. The change was so gradual that it was hard to pinpoint at first. We thought he was still recovering from the virus and took him to the doctor. But, slowly, we became aware that things were getting worse. He seemed to have lost his sparkle — he used to be such a lively, interested and interesting 10-year-old, with a passion for Arsenal! Then even football lost its charm for him. We felt he was just going through the motions of everyday life. He would agree to most things, but do them without enjoyment. He quickly became tearful over minor incidents. He stayed indoors more and more, and we realised that he spoke less frequently about his friends or their joint activities. Unless we pushed him into doing some activity, he would just do nothing. It was such an upsetting difference from the energetic, sometimes exhausting, lively child that we had known."

The teacher

Angela is an eight-year-old, intelligent girl whom her teacher thought of as a "real pain" in the classroom. In a reasonably well behaved class of 32 children, she was very much the odd one out. Some of the other children, especially the boys, were amused by the way she made peculiar noises when the class was supposed to be quiet, but most of the others, like her teacher, were irritated by the way she drew attention to herself. Angela, when not being disruptive, would sit looking out of the window, apparently in a world of her own. In the playground she would mix with a group of young children, sometimes pushing them around and hurting them, so that teachers had to intervene. Although Angela's mother had previously denied any problem with her at home, on the next occasion the teacher saw her she decided to press more firmly on the subject. Eventually tears came to Angela's mother's eyes and she explained how her husband had been made redundant, was drinking heavily, and was himself depressed. Money was very, very tight. Angela was his favourite of the four children, but now he had little time for her and would push her away when she tried to sit on his knee. The mother herself was worried about Angela, who was not at all naughty at home, but miserable and listless, not wanting to play with her friends, and sometimes saying she wished she were dead.

At the teacher's suggestion, through her general practitioner, Angela was referred to the local child and family psychiatric clinic. The family members were seen together on three occasions and Angela's father was able to talk about his sense of failure. The family problems remained considerable, but Angela now seemed to understand the situation, was more settled and less miserable, wanted to play with her friends and was much less trouble in class.

The teenager

Anna was a 14-year-old girl who described her depression very movingly.

"I felt as though no one could like me. I began to wonder just what was the point of anything. At first I lost interest in everything. I felt tired all the time and didn't sleep properly. I would wake up before the rest of the family and lie there feeling grotty and forgotten by the whole world. It felt as if everything was darkness and full of nothing, stretching out to the horizon and filling every corner."

When adults look back on their childhood, they sometimes describe clear episodes of depression. Sir Peter Hall, the theatre director and founder of the Royal Shakespeare Company, describes in his autobiography, *Making an Exhibition of Myself* (Sinclair-Stevenson, London, 1994) how he has, from time to time in his life, become suicidally depressed. On the first occasion he was eight years old. His family had moved from a small village to what seemed to him the big city of Cambridge. He writes:

> "I have felt suicidal several times . . . this was the first time it struck and perhaps because I had fewer inner resources and less to distract me than when I was grown up, it was perhaps the worst time of all. I was very near the brink . . . I was sent to the elementary school just around the corner . . . I, an only child of eight and a loner from the wilds of Suffolk, was mocked by brawling boys and giggling girls. Perhaps it was because of my Suffolk burr. I remember how the children listened to me and then burst out laughing . . . My depression was acute and today would be considered very dangerous. I survived, as I was always to survive, by frantic activity. I gradually came back from the brink."

Sylvia Plath, the poet who committed suicide in 1962 in her early 30s, wrote in one of her last poems, *Lady Lazarus*:

> "I have done it again
> One year in every ten
> I manage it —
>
> A sort of walking miracle . . .

> I am only thirty.
> And like the cat I have nine times to die.
>
> This is Number Three . . ."

(from *Ariel*, published by Faber & Faber, London, 1965)

It is clear that Sylvia Plath had depressive episodes in which she at least contemplated and maybe attempted suicide at the age of ten years.

We should make it clear there is no evidence that people who are very creative are more likely to suffer depression than others. But they have their share of depression, and when they are affected they are, of course, particularly good at describing what it feels like.

Attitudes to depressed children

So children and teenagers *do* get depressed. Parents and teachers, when they hear about a child who might be depressed, think to themselves "They're just too young for that to happen". But, as you can see from these examples, they are certainly not too young. It is not helpful to deny that the young can get depressed. That attitude usually means that we close our eyes and pretend that it is not happening even when it clearly is.

Another attitude can be summed up as "Oh, how awful, poor thing. It upsets me terribly just to think about it. How dreadful for the parents. How guilty they must be." That is not very helpful either. Depressed children and teenagers do need sympathy, but this is not enough. Furthermore, although troubles at home are sometimes the cause of depression, there are many other causes, some in school (as Peter Hall's example shows) and some in the child's or teenager's personality.

Depression in childhood and early adolescence is a fact of life we have to face. It *is* sad, but there is often a good deal that can be done to help, providing we recognise that the problem exists, and providing that we do not jump to conclusions too quickly about what is causing it.

In this book we have tried to provide useful information about depression in the young. It is, in fact, one of the most common, serious problems in today's school-age population. We have tried to describe the ways that depression can be recognised by parents, teachers and the young themselves. We then explain what can be done to help.

1   What is depression?

Everyone recognises that children and young people of any age can be sad and miserable. Disappointments and frustrations, some big and some small, are common in the lives of the young. Furthermore, we all recognise that when sadness and misery are prolonged, children and teenagers can be really quite distressed. However, it is only relatively recently, in the past 20 years or so, that it has become clear that a significant number of children and teenagers (see Chapter 3) have such serious disturbances of mood that it is quite appropriate to think of them as having depressive disorders.

Although depression in a child or teenager may sometimes be best seen as a disorder or even an illness, this is by no means the only way to look at it. Depression in a young person may be a sign that something is very wrong in the family or the school or in the neighbourhood. Social, educational, and family perspectives on depression are sometimes more appropriate than seeing

it as a disorder or a medical problem. We hope this will become clear after we have described the ways depression in the young can occur.

Every 10 or 15 years the World Health Organization publishes guidelines for doctors, psychologists and nurses on the ways in which it is internationally agreed that diagnoses should be made. In the latest version, published in 1992, there is guidance that depression in childhood and adolescence should be diagnosed in the same way as in adults. Obviously the sorts of stresses of children and young people are different from those found in adults, but in our experience, the World Health Organization is right. Although the stresses are different, the ways in which children, young people and adults show depression are really very similar — not identical, but in many ways the same.

2   Signs of depression

Sad, unhappy mood

The child or young person with depression will show sadness and misery for weeks at a time, with little variation from day to day, although the mood may change during the day. Even though circumstances may alter, the sad mood may persist.

Recognising a persistently unhappy mood may not be easy. The boy or girl may experience a mood change, but not want to admit it. As we describe below, children and young people who are depressed may have other problems, such as difficult, disobedient or even aggressive behaviour. It is particularly hard for parents and teachers to recognise persistently sad mood in a child who is being disruptive. By no means all disruptive, difficult children are depressed, but a sizeable number of them are.

Depression is sometimes also accompanied by anxiety, and this may show itself with aches and pains, especially stomach-aches and headaches which are difficult to diagnose. If a parent is worried that there may be something physically wrong with the child, the accompanying depressed mood may well be overlooked.

Lack of pleasure in ordinary, everyday activities

Most children and teenagers will say that they get bored sometimes. They usually mean they get bored when there is nothing to do, when, for example, their friends are away or do not call for them, or when the weather is bad and they cannot play football, or when the computer has broken. Such 'boredom' is not usually a sign of depression. It *is* a sign when young people have the opportunity to do things they normally enjoy, but do not want to participate. That is the time to worry. Friends do call around, but they do not want to have anything to do with them. They show no interest in PE at school, although this is usually their favourite lesson. If children and teenagers show a change in their behaviour in this way over some weeks, this is a clear warning sign of depression.

Disturbed sleep

This can show itself in a number of ways. Difficulty getting off to sleep, waking in the night, being unable to get back to sleep, and waking much earlier than usual in the morning are quite common. Persistent, unhappy and troubling dreams are less common but may occur. So may sleepwalking and sleep-talking, but these are even less common.

How does one know if a child is getting enough sleep? Tiredness and lack of energy during the day are signs of this. On the other hand, the fact that a child will not go to sleep when parents think he or she should is not necessarily a sign of depression, or, indeed, of anything at all being wrong with the child. Some children and teenagers do genuinely have less need for sleep than most. The child who has a lot of energy during the day is probably getting enough sleep, although parents might wish they saw less of him or her in the late evenings!

Changes in appetite

Some children with depression become very picky and go off their food. Others turn to food for comfort and

eat far more than is healthy. Either way, if there is a persistent change in attitude towards food, this is a worrying sign.

Dieting is common, especially in teenage girls, and if all girls who went on diets were depressed, there would only be a few who escaped it! It is the girl who does not enjoy food who is much more likely to be depressed. And most girls who diet feel exactly the opposite about their food.

If a girl diets to an excessive degree because she is preoccupied with her appearance, when she is, in fact, of perfectly normal weight, or even underweight, then she is probably suffering from anorexia or is likely to do so. That is also a cause of great concern. Some girls (and occasionally boys) with anorexia also show signs of depression, but this is not usually the case.

Suicidal thoughts or behaviour

Without doubt, this is the most worrying of all the signs of depression, and rightly so. Every year probably something like one in a hundred 12 to 16-year-olds make a suicide attempt. (That will mean 10 students in a secuondary school with about 1000 students on the roll.) About 1 in 7 deaths in the 15 to 19-year age group

is due to suicide. Fortunately, both suicide and attempted suicide are very much less common under the age of 13 or 14 years, but they do occur.

Not all children who have suicidal ideas are depressed. Fleeting thoughts that life is not worth living are really quite common in the young without depression. A child who stamps a foot when denied a favourite television programme, and says "All right, I'll kill myself" may just be copying behaviour seen on some other television programme. And, if the child is out playing with friends half an hour later, this is likely to be the case. Furthermore, some children who make suicide attempts, or even commit suicide, are not depressed. They may be angry and impulsive youngsters, or perfectionists fearful of failure and faced by an ordeal which they think may be beyond them. But there is no doubt that depression is an important underlying factor in many suicide attempts. Any indication of suicidal intention must be taken very seriously.

Recognising that a youngster has persistent suicidal thoughts is often not an easy matter. Numerous surveys have revealed that parents are usually quite unaware of whether their teenage children have these thoughts, and it is not at all uncommon for them to be able to cover up from their parents when they have actually made a suicide attempt. Obviously, if children show depression

ah... a Study in BLACK.

in the other ways described here, it is important to consider the possibility that they may have suicidal ideas. Remarks by a child or a teenager that they are feeling hopeless or that life is not worth living should be taken seriously. Indeed, persistent hopelessness about the future and a view of the future as bleak and unpleasurable are further signs of depression.

With younger children their play may reveal how they are feeling. Play with dolls that constantly repeats themes of separation from parents; dangerous or reckless play; destructive play; and play that constantly involves life-endangering themes — all these may indicate that even quite a young child of six or seven years has suicidal ideas.

Of course a lot of children, especially boys, will be taken up with fantasy figures like Superman, whose life is constantly in danger, and when deciding if a boy's play is really a sign of depression, one needs to think about whether there are other signs of depression.

It is difficult for parents and teachers to accept that a teenager may be having suicidal ideas. For a parent, particularly parents who have themselves had suicidal ideas, and who are under stress, the additional load of such thoughts in their child may be just too much to bear. For a teacher stressed by demands made, for example, by the National Curriculum and perhaps other problems at home, the thought that a student might be

suicidal creates possible responsibilities for action it might be easier not to take. For a friend, there will be the guilt of not recognising a "best friend's" distress. Yet the recognition of suicidal thoughts in a depressed teenager may be a life-saving achievement.

> When Sue, at 15 years old, attempted suicide by taking an overdose, her best friend was stunned. "I didn't know anything was wrong with her. Yes, I realised she had been a bit weepy and unhappy recently, but I just put it down to 'that time of the month'. When the class heard that she'd tried to kill herself they were freaked out. Some of them reacted by calling her a nutter and then not wanting anything to do with her. But a few of us were really tearful because we were frightened that we would end up doing the same thing, and maybe no one would succeed in stopping us."

Teachers need to be aware of the copycat effect which sometimes arises following a pupil's attempted or successful suicide. Discussions in the classroom can be helpful. It is useful to allow time for each child to express feelings about what has happened, about the loss of a school friend, whether they feel guilty that they could, somehow, have stopped it. One should be particularly sensitive with more vulnerable children who may be experiencing similar feelings and anxieties.

Self-blame

Depressed children and teenagers are likely to take the troubles of their families, their friends and even the world in general on their own shoulders. They tend to be perfectionists and have very high standards for themselves. They may blame themselves for arguments their parents have, for the separation of their parents, for an illness in a brother or sister. Reassurance that they are not responsible may fail to convince them.

Self-blame is not one of the more common signs of depression in children and teenagers, but it does occur. Again, talking with them about the stressful events in their lives may reveal these ideas. With younger children their playing or drawings may show how badly they feel about their lives, and how they feel they deserve to be punished for things they have not done.

More commonly, there is a loss of self-esteem. The child or youngster just has a very poor view of him- or herself. Low self-esteem and depression are very closely linked, although they are not identical. Occasionally a child may have one without the other.

Other signs

In thinking about whether a child or teenager is depressed, the presence of any of the problems described here should be regarded as a warning sign. But there are other issues to bear in mind. Has there been a change in the child's normal behaviour? A child who is happy not to see friends more than occasionally is different from a sociable child who gradually stops wanting to see friends. How is the child's everyday life affected? The child who is functioning really well despite the presence of these problems is less a cause for concern than a child who is, for example, unable to do schoolwork, losing weight, or missing school activities.

Is the child's 'depression' a normal response to a recent serious loss? If father has just left home, or a teenage girl has broken off a relationship with a long-standing boyfriend, many of the above problems may be present for several weeks, and that would be quite normal. But if the child's mood remains constantly depressed for longer, this is a real cause for concern.

It is not always easy to distinguish depression from understandable distress. But in some ways it is not all that important to do so. If a child or teenager remains depressed or distressed, whatever you like to call it, over several weeks, there is reason to be worried and to want to do something about it. Suicidal thoughts and suicidal behaviour are a major cause for concern, whatever one calls the problem underlying it, and however severe or apparently trivial the disappointment or loss the child has experienced.

Psychotic depression

If this were a book about depression in adults, we would need to spend some time on this subject. Fortunately, psychotic depressive illnesses are rare in children and adolescents under the age of 16 years, but they do very occasionally occur, so we must mention them briefly. Nearly all teenagers show mood swings to some degree, but some get very depressed and then in other phases are unusually cheerful, talkative and energetic. In a small proportion of these, very worrying changes occur.

The main special features are delusions (false ideas that cannot be changed even though they are obviously wrong) and hallucinations (usually hearing voices or seeing things that are not there). These psychotic symptoms are often accompanied by a dramatic slowing up of movement and speech. The child may also refuse, or not be able, to eat. Sometimes these psychotic episodes alternate with unusually cheerful moods of over-excitement and over-talkativeness. This is called a bipolar disorder. However, such 'hypomanic' episodes may not occur, and there may just be repeated episodes of severe depression. The disorder is then called unipolar.

Treatment involves counselling and support, medication, and, very, very occasionally, electroconvulsive therapy (see p. 48).

It needs to be emphasised that this type of problem is very rare indeed in those under 16 years. When it does occur, however, it always needs specialist treatment.

Chronic fatigue

Persistent tiredness and lack of energy are important signs of depression. When these are the most prominent problems, someone may diagnose the child or teenager as having myalgic encephalomyelitis (ME) or postviral fatigue syndrome. This form of illness sometimes follows a viral or flu-like illness. The child shows extreme fatigue after exercise, for example. The problem may be prolonged, lasting weeks or even months. The disorder has much in common with depression — in particular it often has physical and psychological components. It usually responds to gentle rehabilitation, and this can sometimes best be provided by a specialist psychiatric team.

Associated problems

Children and young people who are depressed often have other mental health problems and these may be very prominent, so that the depression is masked by them unless it is thought about. The most common associated problem is excessive anxiety and worrying. Indeed, these are so commonly associated that some people think they are part of the same condition. Anxiety is often focused around separation from parents, illnesses or possible death in parents who are, in fact, quite healthy, particular lessons in school, examinations, losing friends — the list is endless.

Another set of problems commonly linked to depression is difficult, aggressive behaviour. Children and young people who are disobedient, rebellious, verbally and sometimes physically abusive, may also be depressed. It is difficult to talk to them about depression because they want to keep their veneer of toughness, but it is sometimes possible.

When children are very troublesome, it is always worthwhile asking oneself if they are not also very unhappy. Just sometimes, showing a difficult child that one has recognised how sad he or she is may provide the first opportunity for real lines of communication to be established.

The bully

John, at just eight years old, was the class bully. He was openly disliked, not only by his peer group, but by many of the children in the other classes. Disruptive and aggressive both in class and the playground, teachers had great trouble managing him and he was eventually referred to an educational psychologist. It was evident to the psychologist that John had a number of cuts, bruises and scratches, which he claimed were accidental — he actually said he was accident-prone. Asked about his interests, John talked about the TV series *The Borrowers*. But, unlike other children, he talked about the little people's smallness and vulnerability, rather than any of their exploits. He recounted stories of them being swept away by the washing-up water, or being under threat in various ways, for example from the cat. It emerged that he felt small and helpless, like the tiny Borrowers, and hit out in a desperate attempt to assert himself against what felt like an overwhelming, threatening and uncaring world. Subsequently, he admitted to hurting himself deliberately when frustrated and feeling particularly unloved and unwanted.

Another commonly linked set of problems are the eating disorders, especially anorexia nervosa in girls, and very occasionally in boys. Persistent dieting behaviour may be only part of their difficulties.

Finally, and often overlooked because such children are often seen as beyond help, is the link between heavy alcohol consumption and drug consumption and depression. It is surprising to some people that the *average* weekly consumption of alcohol in 11-year-old boys is six units, and in 15-year-old boys is seven units, the equivalent of three and a half pints of beer. Quite a few drink much more than this. The rate increases quite sharply with age. Young people who drink heavily or who take drugs may get depressed because they run into financial problems and cannot afford the habits they have developed. The effects of alcohol and other substance abuse often produce depression in themselves. Alternatively, some teenagers develop a drug or alcohol habit because they are seriously depressed and find drink or drugs help to remove intolerable black moods. Either way, the teenager who is depressed and who also has a drink or drug problem is in trouble and will need help.

MAKES ME FEEL GOOD - O.K.?

3 How common is depression in children and young people?

About 2 in 100 children under the age of 12 are depressed to the extent that they would benefit from seeing a specialist child psychiatrist. However, about another 4 or 5 in every 100 of this age show significant distress and some of these could be described as on the edge of depression. The rate goes up with age, so that about 5 in a 100 teenagers are seriously depressed, and at least twice that number show significant distress. These figures apply to children living in stable, settled populations in reasonably good social circumstances. In troubled, inner-city areas with high rates of broken homes, poor community support and raised neighbourhood crime rates, the level of depression may be twice the figures we have quoted. About 6 in every 100 000 15 to 19-year-old boys and 1 to 2 per 100 000 girls commit suicide each year in the UK. The rates are much lower in 10 to 14-year-old children, and under 10 years suicide is very rare. Attempted suicide is much

more frequent, especially in girls, and as many as 2 or 3 girls in every 100 make a suicide attempt at some time during their teenage years. Usually they take tablets. The seriousness of attempts varies a good deal.

These figures relating to depression and suicide mean that in a secondary school in a reasonably settled area, with 1000 children on the roll, about 50 children will be depressed in any one year. In a primary school with about 400 children on the roll in an inner-city area, about eight children will be seriously depressed, and double that number will be significantly distressed. Other children in these schools, and often quite a lot of them, will have problems such as disruptive behaviour and learning difficulties.

Various factors affect the rates of depression, and these are discussed under separate headings below.

Differences between girls and boys

Before puberty, boys and girls suffer depression to a roughly equal degree. After puberty the rate in girls is higher, so that by 15 or 16 years, it is twice as high as in boys. There could be physical, perhaps glandular or genetic reasons for this. It is rather more likely that girls respond to stress with depressive reactions more

Just a RUN OF The mill GiRL.

often than boys do, because they are more emotionally involved in relationships and in other aspects of their lives.

Ethnic differences

There are no clear-cut differences between ethnic groups. In some Third World countries, children and young people are more likely to show physical symptoms when they are depressed than do those living in the more economically developed countries.

Poverty

Poverty and poor social conditions are not, in themselves, causes of depression. However, children living in families where poor home conditions create stress are more likely to be depressed.

Changes over time

Are children more likely to be depressed now than used to be the case 30 or 40 years ago? Research findings suggest the changes have not been marked, but there may have been a rise in the rate of depression. Rates of attempted suicides admitted to hospital among young people, however, went down in the early 1980s, although they are still much too high. Rates of suicide have been stable for some years, except for a recent rise in rates for 15 to 19-year-old boys, and this well may be because of a rise in alcohol consumption and substance abuse in youngsters of this age.

4 What causes depression in children and young people?

Depression in a child does not usually have just one cause. It is useful to think of two broad groups of causes. Like a plant, depression grows because a particular seed (perhaps psychological such as a loss, or perhaps physical such as a viral infection) has been planted in soil which is good for growth. The child's genes or inherited characteristics, the child's personality and the child's early experiences can be seen together as the soil in which the seed is planted. Just as both seed and soil are necessary for plant growth (you won't get much plant unless you have both of these!), so when we look at depression we need to look at both the seeds, or triggering events, and at the nature of the child at the time these events occur. It would be meaningless to say that one or the other is the cause: both are necessary. Let us look at the triggers.

Losses, disappointments and stresses

Loss is an essential part of ordinary growth and development. In fact, it can often be the spur to change and psychological maturity. As we move on to the next stage of life, we have to lose something of the current stage. If we do not let go we cannot move on. Going to school for a child may be exciting, stimulating and open up new social relationships, but it also entails the loss of the all-day familiarity of home, or closeness to parents. Similar losses occur throughout our lives: becoming a sexual teenager, for example, entails loss of childishness.

What helps with all these losses is the belief that there are secure, trusting relationships to turn to. If the child (or adult for that matter) feels basically confident and hopeful in relationships, losses in the 'real', external world are coped with in an optimistic manner.

We all become distressed and some of us become depressed when faced with significant losses and disappointments. Children are no exception. Furthermore, we are all aware that the degree of distress we experience in relation to a loss depends on the emotional significance to us of the person involved. Again, the same is true for children and young people, but, especially with younger children, it may be difficult to know how significant a loss has been.

All the factors below, and quite possibly others, will affect the significance of the loss to the child. A parent or teacher may be surprised at the extent of upset a loss produces in a child because they have not appreciated the importance of one or more of these issues. For the same reason, parents and teachers may be surprised how apparently unscathed the child is by a loss which seemed likely to be devastating.

Let us take just as an example why a child might be more or less upset at 'losing a friend'.

Why has the friend been lost?

If she or he has had a serious illness and died, this will obviously give a different meaning to the loss than if the child has moved away to another school or neighbourhood, or there has been an argument between the two children.

How close is the relationship?

Did the two children do everything together, or was this a friendship just based on an occasional contact?

What causes depression in children and young people?   23

How many other friends does the child have?

The child whose only friend has moved away is in a different position from a child who has five or six other children with whom she or he is friendly.

Was there a sexual component to the relationship?

It is going to be more difficult for a teenager to lose a friendship in which there was some degree of physical attraction and, perhaps, a physical relationship.

Is there any 'unfinished business' in the relationship?

For example, did the children have the opportunity to say goodbye to each other? Or did the child find the friend had disappeared when she or he returned to school at the beginning of a new term, maybe because the friend had moved to another town during the school holidays? Were there any unresolved arguments when the children last saw each other? If so, perhaps the child had a fantasy that the friend went away because she or he was angry.

What, if any, opportunity will there be for contact in the future?

Are the two going to write to each other or speak on the phone? Would that help the child cope with the loss?

Other triggers

When a child becomes depressed beyond a degree that one might call normal distress, it is usually fairly obvious what the trigger is. Sometimes, however, it is quite unclear, and the following list of factors that have been known to act as triggers may be helpful.

- losses — of a parent (through separation or death), a brother or sister, a grandparent or other relative, a friend, an acquaintance, a pet
- disappointments — not going to the school they wanted on school transfer, failing an examination, not doing as well as they hoped in some out-of-school activity (e.g. athletics, ballet, piano), not being able to get to some exciting event, such as a wedding, birthday party, disco

- stresses — arguments in the family (between parents, with one or both parents, with brothers or sisters); pressure to do better at school, a difficult examination, an admission to hospital (or, more importantly, several admissions), bullying at school, violence in the neighbourhood, perhaps related to racism, a physical or mental illness in the child or in someone close to the child
- abuse — clearly, if a child is being violently treated, pressured into unwanted sexual activity, or is being 'put down' or scapegoated a good deal of the time, this is going to act as a serious stress; children react in a variety of ways, of which depression is certainly one
- physical events — a flu-like illness, glandular fever or some other physical illness, an epileptic fit or series of fits.

We have already seen how the same trigger, such as the loss of a friend, can have very different effects in different children. There are three other points which need to be made about triggers.

Firstly, as Claudius in *Hamlet* said, "when sorrows come they come not single spies, but in battalions". The more triggers a child is experiencing, the more he or she is likely to become depressed.

Secondly, when a physical stress occurs, it is sometimes difficult to know whether the depression is caused by physical infection or injury, by the stress of being ill and perhaps being admitted to hospital, or by the worried reactions of parents and family or even perhaps by doctors and nurses creating unnecessary anxiety about symptoms.

Thirdly, and this is more complicated, a child or youngster who is already depressed can create a stress that then misleadingly looks as though it is causing the depression when, in fact, the situation should be looked at the other way around. For example, a depressed child may have difficulties concentrating on school work and therefore fail an important examination. Everyone may think the failure has caused the depression, but this would be misleading.

Brothers and sisters

When a child or adolescent is depressed, she or he usually becomes the focus of attention, and other members of the family are often ignored. It is easy to forget the existence of brothers and sisters. Yet some research has shown that, if a child is depressed, and there are brothers and sisters, more than one in three of them will also be depressed. They need attention too. Indeed, in considering them in addition, the reasons for the first child's depression may become apparent, and ways of helping may become more obvious.

Vulnerability

So much for triggers, or seeds of depression. What about the nature and temperament of the child — the soil into which the seed falls?

Genes and chromosomes

Parents who have had depressive illnesses themselves are, sadly, more likely to have children with depression. That does not mean that all children of depressed parents get depressed too. In fact, most do not, but they do have an increased tendency to do so. Now this could be, and probably partly is, because a depressed parent almost inevitably creates a somewhat stressful environment for the child. A mother who is absorbed with depressed thoughts about the future and feels terrible is going to find it more difficult to provide her child with the necessary warmth, affection and control. However, she is also going to pass on half her genes. Genes are

long strands of protein (DNA) present in every human cell from the time sperm enters the egg, and we are conceived. They dictate whether we are going to be taller or shorter than most people, whether we will develop one of a hundred or more rare diseases, such as cystic fibrosis, or less rare diseases such as Alzheimer's disease in old age. Perhaps genes also have some effect on whether we have an increased likelihood of becoming depressed. Most experts think they do.

Some people think that unless you are born with a particular characteristic, it cannot be inherited, but that cannot be right. After all, puberty occurs around about the ages of 10 to 15 years because we are programmed by our genes that way, not because of events that happen to us. It is quite possible that, at least in some people, depression is partly genetically caused.

There is now a reasonable amount of information from twin studies and from studies of families suggesting this is also the case for some children. But it will probably only be in occasional cases that genes are the most important cause.

In those cases where genes are important, how do they exert their effects? They affect the personality (see below), but they may also alter the way the brain functions in response to stress. A great deal of work has been undertaken to see if chemicals (neurotransmitters) that operate in the brain and the passage of messages between nerve cells are affected in depression. Other work has been undertaken with hormones, particularly steroid hormones that are known to be affected by stress. So far, no conclusive results have appeared, and the role of biochemical factors and glandular secretions in causing childhood depression remains uncertain.

Temperament and personality

One way in which genes can increase the chances of a child becoming depressed is by their effect on moulding the child's personality. As described earlier, the child is born with a given temperament, and this will affect how the care of the parent is experienced by the child, and will in turn affect the quality of care. For instance, a quiet baby with regular body functions such as sleep and feeding will be quite a different baby to care for than a noisy baby who is difficult to satisfy and wakes and feeds irregularly.

If mothers or fathers are anxious, depressed or unsure of themselves, they may not find a way of dealing with the baby that works for them. On the other hand, they may be experienced parents with adequate supports, and rise to the challenge of the more difficult baby in order to help the child feel more secure in the early days.

This early pattern of relating may have longer-term effects in later life. Children who feel understood and in tune with their environment will have a greater inner security and trust that things will work out in the long run. Those who feel the world is at odds with their own needs could well become more pessimistic.

In later years, as they move into school, some children remain easily upset, cry readily and are discouraged by minor disappointments. Such children may be particularly likely to become depressed, and, even more unfortunately, they may even create the circumstances that are likely to produce depression. So, for example, a child with this type of personality can attract bullying at school and thus can, in a sense, be responsible for one of the stresses that can act as a trigger.

Earlier experiences

As we have already suggested, children who are depressed have low self-esteem and a negative view of their past experience. Sadly, many children have every right to consider their past experiences disastrous. Children who have been physically or sexually abused, sometimes on a frequent and regular basis, fall into this category. If they have not been made depressed by their experiences, they are nevertheless prone to depression as they move into adolescence. Children whose early years have been lived under a cloud of physical or mental illness in the family, perhaps an alcohol problem in father or a depressive illness in mother, may have been sensitised to further stress. Unexpected early separations, such as an emergency admission to hospital, may also have made the child vulnerable, so that even a minor further separation may reactivate a worry which is always just below the surface.

Other long-lasting difficulties

Some children suffer from long-lasting difficulties that make them particularly prone to depression. Thus, children with chronic physical disorders, such as diabetes, cystic fibrosis, asthma, and, more especially, epilepsy and cerebral palsy, are at slightly greater risk. The same is true for children with learning difficulties at school. It should be emphasised that most children with these long-lasting difficulties will not be depressed, but they are at slightly greater risk.

Coping skills and protective factors

When a child has to face a disappointment or a stress, she or he is not just a passive individual taking what

comes without the ability to do anything about it. Children and teenagers respond actively to bad experiences in order to try to master and overcome them. These 'coping skills' help to explain why some children do not become depressed, even though faced with terrible adversity. Similarly, some children faced with adversity have positive things going for them in their environment and, if these protective factors are present, they lower the risk of depression in children facing stress. Helpful coping skills include the ability to confide worries to friends and family members, and the capacity to deal with one problem at a time rather than be overwhelmed by a mass of difficulties. Children who have a particularly good relationship with one or both parents; who have someone outside the immediate family, such as a grandparent, in whom they can confide; who have some special skills or a talent for athletics or artistic ability — all these are less likely to develop depression when stressful circumstances strike.

The protective factors and coping skills enjoyed by children and teenagers are important because they sometimes give clues as to how we can best help children under stress. Reinforcing natural strengths is often a better idea than trying to invent completely new methods of treatment to deal with weaknesses.

Understanding the causes of depression is quite complicated if we try to produce a scheme which fits all children. The diagram below is an attempt to bring all these factors together. You will see how some factors push the child or young person towards more serious depression, while others enhance resistance. But, of course, no diagram can do justice to the richness involved in the life of any one particular child.

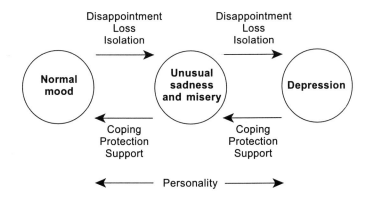

5 Helping the depressed child — what you (parents, teachers, other children) can do

People all need people, as the words of the song go. But when we are sad, distressed or unhappy, we need other people even more — even if we think we do not!

There is a great deal that can be done by parents, teachers and others to help depressed children, and on pages 37 and 38 we provide action sheets for guidance.

Listening

Listening to children sounds so simple and obvious, but sometimes it is the quality of the listening that counts more than anything. It is, in fact, rather difficult to listen to children (or people generally) in distress. There are many reasons why children do not get heard in everyday life. For example, in school, they may be overlooked if:

- they are quiet and withdrawn
- the class is too big and troublesome

- teachers are too tired or worried themselves.

Both parents and teachers may find themselves overlooking depressed children if

- they are too wrapped up in their own problems (perhaps death of a relative or friend, marriage problems, how to make ends meet)
- they feel helpless and useless in the face of someone else's despair
- they are just too busy
- it is too upsetting to think about.

So, it is important to look at *yourself*, to ask whether you are hearing children's distress and to think about what could be done to help you to listen better. Caring for ourselves enables us to care for our children. As a parent, are you depressed yourself? Support, help, advice and even treatment for parents is an important aspect of helping children. (For more on this aspect see *Down with Gloom!* published by Gaskell with the Defeat Depression Campaign and available from the Royal College of Psychiatrists.) It is important not to feel that a child's problems are all your fault, as this, too, may be a block to you listening in a positive way.

Teachers and other professionals may need to look at their practice. Are you overworked — and who is not? Do you need support to think about the multitude of problems presenting in everyday situations? Regular supervision or discussion with someone outside the busy work setting can really help to pick up problems that may otherwise be overlooked.

Aspects of listening

Try listening with the heart and not just the ears. Imagine the child's distress by relating it (in your mind only) to periods of distress in your own life.

Do not belittle the child's unhappiness. Behind every attention-seeker is a real problem that perhaps the child needs to dramatise in order to ensure an audience. If the child does not feel you are taking the problem seriously, you run the risk of the child heightening the drama, and perhaps acting in a self-destructive way.

As a parent, if you think your child is attention-seeking, you need to ask why she or he needs so much attention. What is it that this child is trying to draw attention to?

Time
- give time to listen properly
- minimise external distractions
- take the telephone off the hook
- find a private, secluded room
- do not allow interruptions — these will make the child feel that the problem is just a burden for you and that you do not, after all, have the time and patience to listen properly.

Listen
- do not recount your own worries or upset the child
- do not tell stories about other people's problems
- let the child see that you take the problems and worries seriously, however trivial you may find them
- do not attempt to cheer the child up with phrases like "come on now, it is not the end of the world" or "it may never happen", and so on — it may just feel like the end of the world to this child, since she or he feels that 'it' has already happened
- do not blame the child.

Reflect back

Children feel heard and understood if you summarise what they have said by repeating or putting what they have said in another way. Sometimes it may be necessary to comment on how they look, if they find it difficult to verbalise (e.g. "you do look upset" or "I can see how difficult it is to talk about this").

Drawing or play

Younger children may find it too hard to talk about their feelings. It can be suggested that they draw whatever it is they are feeling, or are worried about. They may express themselves with the help of toys, such as families of dolls and a dolls' house, puppets or toy animals.

Offer hope

Given that despair and hopelessness are features of depression it is useful to think of keeping hope alive for the child. It may help to suggest:

- that these feelings will eventually pass

- that there are ways they can be helped, either through talking or referral to specialists.

Offer practical help

If it is possible to change whatever it was that brought about the depression it should be changed. There may also be practical things that will help, such as arranging for friends to come around, or planning and going on an outing.

However, let us be realistic: by no means everything that brings about a child's depression can be changed. Maybe parents have separated, father has another family and has lost interest in his first children. Maybe mother has a drink problem she is finding it hard to beat. Perhaps the child has a serious physical illness that is chronic, or even progressing. When these problems will not go away, and the child's mood persists, all the other ways of helping — listening, keeping up the support, sharing feelings and so on — become even more important.

But, do not forget, some problems you think cannot go away may be helped to disappear. Not so long ago, for example, many school teachers felt helpless in the face of bullying. They said there was nothing they could do — "boys will be boys" — and girls can be pretty horrible to each other too. But now all schools are expected to have an anti-bullying policy, and much more is indeed being done to prevent this unpleasant aspect of school life.

Keep up the support

Let children know that, until they are feeling better, you are available to them whenever they want to talk to you.

Keep in touch

Do not allow the child to withdraw. This is difficult to achieve without being intrusive. We all know the sullen, uncommunicative teenager who insists that things are all right, and tells you to go away. However, you should:

- keep an eye open, and keep watch at a distance, if that is all they will permit
- persist in expressing your concern from time to time
- do not allow yourself to be fobbed off
- if worried, take it further (see action sheets on pages 37 and 38).

Physical contact

Given possible allegations about sexual abuse involving teachers these days, there is much concern about whether physical contact is appropriate or not. This is a great pity because of a danger that ordinary human empathy and spontaneity could be lost. Sometimes depressed and distressed children need an adult to put an arm around them, to give comfort. It would be sad for this to be denied them. Respond naturally. If a child draws away, do not insist, but continue to talk.

Teachers will be aware of the dangers of having comforting physical contact misinterpreted. This is much less likely to happen if the contact is limited, as it should be, to a briefly held hand contact, a pat on the back or an arm on the shoulder. Misunderstanding is also less likely to occur if there are other people around and they know about how you are attempting to support the child in question.

Confidentiality

Sometimes children will tell a trusted adult, outside their family, of their depression (or suicidal feelings) and insist that this remains a secret. This poses quite a dilemma. How much should the confidentiality be respected; to what extent do parents have a right to know about their child's difficulties? The answer is that parents do have the right to know. And if the situation is severe (as outlined at the start of this chapter), or if the child is at risk of suicide, there is a duty to inform parents.

However, in less worrying situations, it may be possible for, say, a teacher to see a child a few times in order to understand the problem better. It may be that poor communication with the parents is, in fact, part of the problem.

Confidentiality is going to be more of a problem for a teacher when there is suspected abuse at home, perhaps because of something the child has said. In these cases the teacher will talk with the headteacher and a social worker will need to be contacted.

In other circumstances, a joint meeting with the child and parents to air concerns is nearly always helpful.

Seeking professional help

It is important to know, however, when the techniques above are not sufficient, and the child needs specialist help. Professional help should be sought when:

- the depression does not lift after two to three weeks
- there is interference with daily life
- there is severe disturbance of sleep and eating patterns
- there are suicidal thoughts or wishes expressed.

How to get specialist help

Help for problems mainly at home

If the problems are occurring mainly at home and do not improve, then the parents' first port of call should be the family doctor. Most family doctors nowadays see emotional problems in children and teenagers as part of their job, although obviously some are going to be more interested than others (that is true of all professionals). Your doctor will, of course, want to see your child and have a chat with him or her, either with you, separately, or both together. If your child does not want to go to the doctor (and this is not at all unusual) then you, the parent or parents, should go anyway to discuss the situation. You may be in need of help so that you continue to cope, and your doctor may be able to provide assistance here.

Anyway, after seeing you and your child, the doctor will listen, give advice and support, and, just occasionally, prescribe medication. Often there will be a need for further appointments to see how the problem is progressing. If, after several weeks, the problem is no better or even seems to be getting worse, then your doctor will probably suggest a referral to the local child and family psychiatric clinic (discussed in the next chapter). This may have been suggested earlier if the problem is severe. If your doctor does not suggest a referral, then you can suggest one yourself.

Help for problems mainly at school

Once a problem in school has been identified by teachers, parents, or the teenager himself or herself, there needs to be a get-together with everyone (and that 'everyone' includes the child) involved to decide what to do. It will often be helpful for the child to be present from the beginning. Sharing of information in this situation is nearly always going to be useful. If whatever is decided does not prove helpful enough, then a referral should be made, either to the child and family psychiatric clinic, or, if the problem is mainly to do with learning difficulties or behaviour in the classroom, to the educational psychologist attached to the school.

Action sheet for parents

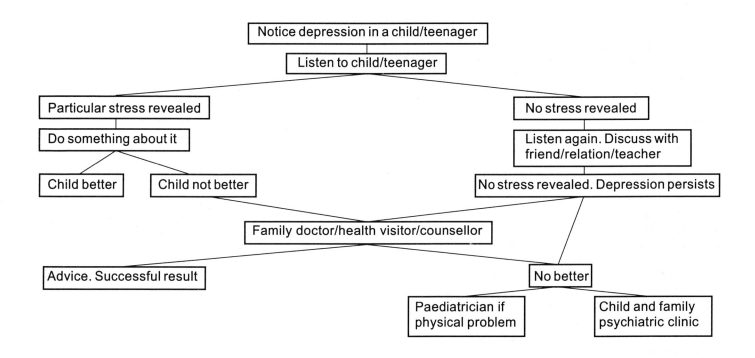

Action sheet for teachers

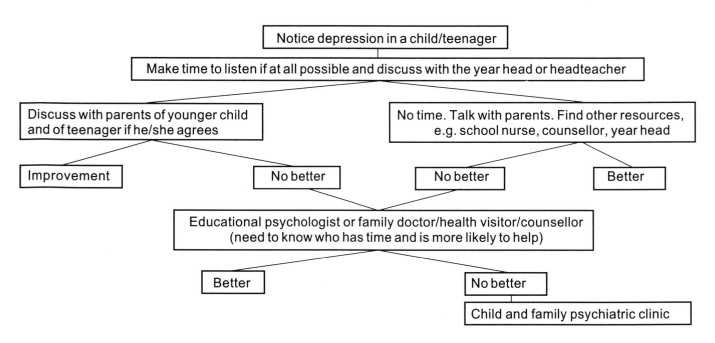

Notice depression in a child/teenager

Make time to listen if at all possible and discuss with the year head or headteacher

Discuss with parents of younger child and of teenager if he/she agrees

No time. Talk with parents. Find other resources, e.g. school nurse, counsellor, year head

Improvement

No better

No better

Better

Educational psychologist or family doctor/health visitor/counsellor (need to know who has time and is more likely to help)

Better

No better

Child and family psychiatric clinic

6   The child and family clinic

Not all clinics have this name. Some are called 'child and family psychiatric clinic', 'family consultation centre', 'child guidance clinic' or 'young people's clinic'. They also differ in where they are placed. Some are in hospital departments, while others are attached to health centres or school premises.

Who works in these clinics?

In most clinics around the country there will be a psychiatrist, social worker, psychologist and community psychiatric nurse, although often not all of these will be present full-time. In and around London there will also often be one or more child psychotherapists, but this would be unusual elsewhere.

A word about the training and background of these professionals is required. Perhaps the most important thing to say is that their skills overlap a good deal. They will all have had training in how to assess emotional problems and in counselling of parents and children. They will all have well developed skills in listening. Often they will also be skilled in a number of different types of therapy, including psychotherapy with individual children and parents, and family therapy.

As well as these skills, they will all have special responsibilities and interests. Social workers have a particular role in child protection work. Of course, this does *not* mean that the first thing they think of would be whether your child needs to be taken away from home. They will want to help parents and children get on better together at home. Social workers have many skills other than in child protection. Psychologists often have special skills in assessing learning difficulties and devising behavioural programmes such as those described under 'Cognitive therapy' below. The community psychiatric nurse will have a background in nursing, and will often be particularly skilled in behavioural management, and with working with families in the home. Psychotherapists have had a long training in individual child psychotherapy, and will have special skills in understanding the 'internal world' of the child. The child and adolescent psychiatrist, who is qualified as a medical doctor, combines a knowledge of the emotional and behavioural problems of children with his or her medical background. It is the child psychiatrist's responsibility to prescribe medication in those unusual cases where this is indicated.

How do the people at the clinic work?

Firstly, there may be a waiting time, and this is likely to be between one month and three months. To save time, the clinic may ask you to provide some information on a questionnaire before you arrive. Often families feel worried about the first appointment letter, which requests the attendance of the whole family. They feel as though the therapist is suggesting that they are to blame in some way for the child's problems. Parents often feel needlessly defensive, and come to the session reluctant to think about what is happening in the family. To begin with, family members are often seen altogether, but later during the assessment they may be seen individually.

Some clinics use one-way screens or video equipment, either for training purposes for staff attached to the clinic who are learning, or because it is felt to be a good way to have more than one view on the problem. If either of these is used, this will be explained to you and your consent will be necessary for its use. You may find this approach too prying and you have every right to withhold consent. However, it can be helpful to those who are trying to understand and help your child and family.

Once the assessment is completed, and this may take anything from an hour to most of the morning or afternoon, the professional or professionals who have seen you will explain what, if any, treatment is being offered. Some families are offered advice on the spot and it is suggested they return if problems persist. In other cases, and in most clinics this is the majority, the child and family is taken on for shorter or longer periods of treatment.

What types of treatment are provided?

Family therapy

So far, we have talked about childhood depression as being a problem located within the child, but this is not always how things are viewed in terms of treatment. Family therapists would want to think about the whole family, not just the person who presents with problems. As we have said above, this is not because the family is felt to be the 'cause' of the problem, but rather because no one member in a family exists in isolation from the others. Family therapists view the problem a child shows as serving a purpose for the family as a whole unit. Thus, a depressed child can be understood only within a set of family relationships, constantly acting upon each other in a circular way. In other words, the problem does not belong to the child, but to the family. The child is showing behaviour in relation to other family members.

> Ian, aged 12 years, and an only child, was brought to a clinic by his parents, who were worried and also exasperated by his depression, lack of interest in activities he previously enjoyed, and feelings of hopelessness. His father did most of the talking,

WHICH ONE OF YOU NEEDS HELP?

explaining how he had tried everything to bring his son out of himself. Ian's mother was silent, but the family therapist felt she was very angry, especially with her husband. It gradually became clear that Ian's father had been made redundant six months previously, and was having no success in finding another job. He was spending much more time with Ian. Previously, Ian's mother had made all the decisions about him, but now she felt pushed out. She had started to argue with her husband about the way he was taking Ian away from his friends to go fishing and to football matches with him. Ian had then started to say he did not want to go out at all. His father then criticised him, and his mother withdrew more. When the situation became clear to the therapist and the parents it was possible for them to argue less about Ian, and his depression lifted, although it did not disappear completely.

Family therapy takes the form of meetings with the entire family (defined as all those who live at home) and the family therapist. These may be limited to an agreed number of sessions (often six to eight), or may be open-ended, over a longer period. Often they occur at fortnightly intervals in order to permit the family to work on things at home between sessions.

Very often the meetings take place in a large room, one wall of which is a one-way mirror. The family therapist may have a co-worker who will observe the session from behind this mirror-screen, in order to gain an independent perspective on the events taking place within the therapy room.

Sometimes the sessions may be videotaped (always with written permission from the parents), so that the therapist may review them at a later stage, perhaps with family members themselves.

Family therapists work through understanding and changing the way family members interact with each other. Very often family trees are drawn within the family sessions to help clarify just what the family tasks are at this stage of the children's lives. Each stage presents the family members with psychological and relationship tasks to perform. Family difficulties may arise at times of change. Other family members also have their own 'lifecycle issues', which will interact with those within the family unit. For example, family life changes when a teenager begins working towards greater independence, and eventually leaves home. The family as a whole is affected. Relationships between the parents will be affected; they have to look to their future together, as a couple again, as their children leave. Loss may be central to the whole family's functioning, and may be associated with grandparents becoming elderly or dying.

The great advantage of family therapy is that it allows for improved communication, especially when family members have things they find difficult to talk about without help. The therapist will therefore be particularly interested to hear family members who have difficulty in making their thoughts and feelings known.

Family therapy is not interested in 'blame', and not even concerned with causes, but works by understanding just how the family is working together. The whole family is affected by a difficulty, and can in turn affect the resolution of it.

Individual psychotherapy with the child

In those places where there is a child psychotherapist on the staff, this is often the person who will provide this form of treatment. Often, however, children are seen individually by other members of the team. Child psychotherapy offers help to the child in his or her own right. The therapist will always keep family issues in mind, and may work with another professional who will see the parents, and sometimes the family, while the child is in psychotherapy. Sometimes the therapist will do this family liaison themselves.

Psychotherapists take the view that much depression is caused by emotions and thoughts which the child or teenager finds difficult to bring to the surface. The psychotherapists help the child to do this through play, drawing or discussion.

In order to develop the therapeutic relationship it is important for the psychotherapist to provide a reliable and consistent setting. Appointments are therefore offered at regular intervals, often once a week or occasionally more frequently.

What happens

Psychotherapy takes place in a private room — always the same room, with the same toys and furniture. The therapist and child meet one to one. The child may be encouraged to find expression in playing with toys or in drawing. Often however, especially with older children, treatment is entirely through talking.

The following examples show how two depressed boys had reacted quite differently to the development of diabetes. Both boys reacted against the diabetic treatment, and would not become involved in planning either a diet or insulin regime. Both became withdrawn and their school work deteriorated.

Steven was only interested in sport, both playing it and watching it. His increased activity led to further problems with control of his diabetes. During psychotherapy it emerged that he had great anxieties about the loss of control over his body. He felt that all the injections had damaged his body's ability to hold together — as if his skin was punctured all over and could not hold him in.

Darren's worries were quite different. He was primarily concerned about feeling different from other people. He had particular difficulty in feeling that he could grow up to be an active and effective man, because he felt that he was so unlike his healthy father.

Once these issues were uncovered and addressed in therapy, both boys were able to partake in their diabetic control and thus settle down again to ordinary life.

Psychotherapy is helpful for those children whose emotional development has been held up or has become stuck in some way. For some children, changes within the family, or the lifting of pressures upon them, are not enough to help them overcome their complex feelings. Psychotherapy focuses on the hopelessness and despair that a depressed child feels, and the therapist tries to understand with them what happens when they are depressed. However, it looks not only at problem areas but at the child's whole personality and coping strategies.

A depressed child will gradually develop a relationship with the therapist through play, drawing or talking. In this way the therapist and child explore together how the child copes with life. The psychotherapist will help the child develop an understanding of his or her feelings, and how these affect behaviour and relationships. This may involve exploring how past experiences and relationships affect the child's ways of coping in the present. The therapist will not suggest solutions to children's difficulties, feeling that it is better for them to strengthen their own ability to reason and work out alternatives for themselves, rather than depend on the therapist. Psychotherapy is a gradual process during which children are allowed to explore their depression. The therapist acknowledges what the child is going through, and this empathy and expression of feeling brings relief. It enables the child to move on, psychologically, to discover new strengths and coping abilities.

In the process of therapy children will experience a whole range of feelings towards the therapist, which is both healthy and expected. This does mean that sometimes a child will become reluctant to come to therapy. It can be hard for parents to continue to bring them and they will need encouragement to help the child to continue to come and express these negative feelings. It is particularly important in depression that angry and aggressive feelings which may arise are brought to the surface. It is a relief to the child to discover that these negative feelings can be tolerated and expressed.

Therapists do not usually suggest to children what to do or how to express themselves. They will often wait to see what children bring up. In this way psychotherapists believe they are dealing with the child's concerns, not imposing the therapist's agenda on the child. Children are free to play, draw, talk or paint as they wish, with the therapist going along with their way of communicating. Given this 'permission', the expectation is that important feelings will be brought to the surface that the child can be helped to understand. This, in itself, will bring about improvement.

Cognitive therapy

Depression can also be seen as a disorder of thinking, and we have already described how some children and teenagers blame themselves, when they have not done anything wrong. If we think we have done something wrong in the past, or the future is hopeless, we may become depressed — our mood follows our thoughts.

And if these ideas are false, our mood is inappropriate and undeserved. So, people who use cognitive therapy argue, helping a depressed child or teenager to think differently and more accurately about his or her past, present or future will also help lift the depression.

Although there are certain similarities, this is quite a different approach to that taken by psychoanalytic therapists, who tend to think of inaccurate thoughts and ideas as following mood rather than the other way around.

How do cognitive therapists, and they may be psychologists or psychiatrists, work? First, the child is asked to explain what she or he means by words like 'angry', 'happy', 'worried', 'cheerful', 'sad', and 'depressed', and to give some examples of when she or he recently experienced these. The child is also asked to describe thoughts and ideas at the time of these experiences. Next, she or he is asked to keep a diary of moods and the thoughts accompanying them. Following this, the child is asked to try to make links between thoughts and the moods that go with them. One or two tasks may then be set, and it is suggested that the child will feel happier when the task is accomplished.

The child will face difficult situations. It is suggested she or he thinks of different solutions and chooses one of them. For example, a boy may be faced with a bully at school and helped to choose whether to tell a teacher, his parents, work out ways of avoiding the bully, talk to other boys about ways of avoiding the bully, and so on. A girl may be helped to examine whether ideas that people are against her or think little of her are accurate, and encouraged to check such ideas against reality. Improved social relationships can be linked to improved mood states.

Specific techniques such as role play with the therapist can sometimes help to make change easier for the child. As time goes on the child is encouraged to challenge previous assumptions that events around him or her have a negative significance. For example, a child may be helped to see that a mother's bad moods are not caused by the child's behaviour, but have all sorts of other reasons. The core of the treatment involves self-monitoring and problem-solving at a conscious level.

Group therapy

In a small number of clinics, children are sometimes treated together in groups of roughly the same age. They may be mixed in terms of sex, although sometimes they are single-sex groups. There will be one or two therapists present.

The group may be focused around a particular subject, with a set agenda, or be less directive and have an open agenda. Group leaders may direct the children into specific activities, aiming to work on particular issues such as cooperation and sharing, or they may let the children decide on the activity and issues together. Sometimes video equipment is used to help the children observe themselves in order to encourage change. Again, written permission from the parents is necessary.

Such groups usually meet once a week, or fortnightly. They may run over a short number of agreed sessions or be more open-ended, depending on the way the group itself develops, in order to decide length or content.

Physical treatments

Physical treatments are usually less important in depressed children and young people than the treatments mentioned above, but they are sometimes helpful and, very occasionally, it turns out that they are the most important part of treatment.

Medication

When the problems of a child or adolescent are severe and do not respond to psychological talking treatments, a doctor, by this time often a child psychiatrist, will consider the possible use of medication.

There are two main groups of antidepressant medication. For many years the so-called tricyclic

antidepressants, especially amitriptyline and imipramine, have been used with depressed children. During the last ten years, numerous excellent studies have been carried out with this form of medication. Unfortunately, it is now clear that, in helping depression in the younger age group, they are only occasionally effective, although they sometimes may be worth trying. They do help symptoms of anxiety and improve sleep, and that can make a difference. They also have occasional side-effects, such as a dry mouth and dizziness when standing up. If this medication is prescribed, it is important it is taken regularly in adequate dosage, over three weeks, because the drugs usually do not start to work for about ten days.

New forms of antidepressants, the so-called serotonin re-uptake inhibitors, have not yet been fully assessed for effectiveness in children, but it is clear that they can be prescribed without serious side-effects, and occasionally they are indeed helpful.

With both these forms of medication, it is important to make sure tablets are kept well out of the way of a teenager who might be suicidal, and preferably locked up. Of course, that also applies to tablets which may be taken by other members of the household. It is particularly important to keep them locked well away from toddlers, who may mistake them for sweets.

Another form of medication, lithium carbonate, is used very occasionally in older children and teenagers who have marked mood swings (see earlier section on psychotic depression). This medication, which is used to prevent attacks of depression, has to be carefully monitored. The teenager has to have regular blood checks to make sure the level of lithium is kept within certain limits.

Electroconvulsive therapy

Electroconvulsive therapy (ECT) is used for children and youngsters up to the age of 16 years very rarely indeed, and its use at all with this group is very controversial. But just very occasionally, for really sick children, perhaps in a depressive coma, refusing food, deluded and hearing voices telling them to end their life, it may be life-saving. (Again, see earlier section on psychotic depression.) A survey in 1991 showed that only two or three children under the age of 16 were treated with ECT each year. No cases are known of children under 12 years currently receiving ECT in the UK.

Other forms of therapy

There are various other specialist forms of treatment for depression that are used from time to time. For example, there are many other sorts of ways in which children can be helped to express their feelings, such as art, drama and music therapies. Hypnosis is another example. Occasionally dietary treatment, involving the removal of certain additives or foods from the diet, is used. These forms of treatment are often applied by very enthusiastic practitioners and it may be that much of their success is due to this fact. It should be said that the more orthodox forms of treatment are also more likely to work if the therapist is keen and motivated.

How is a particular treatment selected?

The treatment the child needs will be chosen for a number of reasons. If there are stresses in school or the home, these will naturally be tackled first. Beyond this, when the problem is mainly seen as within the child, individual therapy of some type is likely to be chosen. Where the problem is thought to be in the way family members interact, then family therapy will be the treatment of choice. Other important considerations include the availability of particular treatment types, and the sort of treatment with which the therapist is most experienced. If parents feel unhappy with a particular form of treatment they are offered, they should not hesitate to raise the matter with a member of the staff of the clinic or with their own doctor.

7 What happens to depressed children and young people?

What happens to depressed children and young people depends very much on the severity of the problem.

The good news is that distressed and mildly depressed children can be expected to improve over several weeks or months, especially if their problems are recognised, sources of unhappiness are dealt with, and they receive sympathetic help.

On the other hand, follow-up studies suggest that more serious forms of depression in children and adolescents (especially those accompanied by marked interference with daily life and persistent suicidal thoughts) do not fare as well. Perhaps as many as a half will go into adult life with a high likelihood of recurrence and the development of further depressive disorders.

Sadly, depression when it occurs in a severe form in childhood or the teenage years is often by no means a passing phase. The good news, however, is that children even with quite serious depression are not at unusual risk of the development of other mental disorders such as schizophrenia. All this means that a number of youngsters with depression, once they have been identified and recognised, will need help over several months and years. It goes without saying that their parents and any brothers or sisters will also need support. Having a severely depressed child in the family is a major load on family life.

We hope, however, that we have made it clear that there is always much that can be done to help a depressed child or teenager, as well as other members of the family. Most children who are distressed or depressed will, fortunately, improve with time, sympathy, and sometimes more expert help.

Further reading

Burningham, S. (1994) *Young People under Stress: A Parent's Guide*. Virago.

Coleman, J. *Teenagers under Stress: An Audio Tape*. Trust for the Study of Adolescents, 23 New Road, Brighton, East Sussex BN1 1WZ.

Lask, B. (1985) *Children's Problems: A Parent's Guide to Understanding and Tackling Them*. Macdonald Optima.

Pearce, J. *Growth and Development*. Thorsons.

Pitt, B. (1993) *Down with Gloom! or How to Defeat Depression*. Gaskell/Royal College of Psychiatrists.

Treadwell, P. (1988) *A Parent's Guide to the Problems of Adolescence*. Penguin.

Understanding Your 5-Year-Old to *Understanding Your 11-Year-Old*. Series of books focusing on each year of life. Rosendale.

Children and Young People Get Depressed Too. Young Minds Information Service (for address see p. 54).

Worried About a Young Person's Eating Problems? Young Minds Information Service.

Notes on the authors

Philip Graham was formerly Professor of Child Psychiatry at the Institute of Child Health and the Hospital for Sick Children, Great Ormond Street, London. He is now attached to the Department of Psychiatry in the University of Cambridge, and is Chair of the National Children's Bureau.

Carol Hughes is a consultant child psychotherapist who trained with the British Association of Psychotherapists. She currently works at King's College Hospital (employed by the Maudsley Hospital), and at ISP, Sittingbourne, Kent.

Note on Defeat Depression Campaign

**Defeat
Depression**

The Defeat Depression Campaign is a five-year national campaign organised by the Royal College of Psychiatrists, in association with the Royal College of General Practitioners. This is an important initiative designed to increase awareness and improve understanding of depression in the community, so that those suffering from this common and disabling illness will not be afraid to seek and receive appropriate treatment. The Campaign aims to change the situation by enhancing the diagnostic and management skills of family doctors and other health professionals, and by educating the general public in the signs and symptoms of depression and the availability of effective treatments.

The Defeat Depression Campaign has launched a series of initiatives for the general public. A selection of leaflets and factsheets have been produced on depression, depression in the elderly, postnatal depression, depression in ethnic minorities, and depression in the workplace. Gaskell Publications have also issued a publication entitled *Down with Gloom! or How to Defeat Depression* by Professor Brice Pitt, with drawings by Mel Calman. This book is available from the Royal College of Psychiatrists at a cost of £3.50.

For further details about the Campaign, please write to the Defeat Depression Campaign Secretariat, 17 Belgrave Square, London SW1X 8PG.

Helpful addresses

All these will provide information and advice.

Association for Child Psychology and Psychiatry, 70 Borough High Street, London SE1 1XF (tel. 0171 403 7458).

British Psychological Society, St Andrew's House, 48 Princess Road East, Leicester, LE1 7DR (tel. 01533 549568)

Childline (confidential helpline for children and young people), Freepost 1111, London EC4B 4BB (tel. 0800 1111, 24-hours, free).

National Children's Bureau, 8 Wokley Street, London EC1V 7QE (tel. 0171 843 6000).

Trust for the Study of Adolescence, 23 New Road, Brighton BN1 1WZ (tel. 01273 693311).

Young Minds, 22a Boston Place, London NW1 6ER (tel. 0171 724 7262).

Your local library will have details of your nearest child and family psychiatric clinic. Most of these will see self-referrals, although they prefer you to have a letter from your doctor.

Index

abuse 25, 28, 34
aggressive behaviour 16–17
alcohol consumption 18, 21
amitriptyline 48
anorexia 10, 17
antidepressant medication 47–48
anxiety 8, 16
appetite changes and disorders 9–10, 17
art therapy 48
assessment 40
associated problems 16–18
asthma 29
attention-seeking behaviour 32
attitudes to depressed children 3–4
bipolar disorder 15
boredom 8
boys, incidence of depression 19–21
brothers 26
bullying 17, 28, 33–34
causes of depression 22–30
cerebral palsy 29

child and family psychiatric clinic 36, 39–49
child guidance clinic 36, 39–49
chromosomes 26–28
chronic illness 29
clinics 36, 39–49
cognitive therapy 45–46
community psychiatric nurses 39–40
confidentiality 34–35
coping skills 29–30
copycat effect and suicide 13
cystic fibrosis 29
Defeat Depression Campaign 53
delusions 15
diabetes 29, 45
diagnosing depression 5–6
dietary therapy 49
dieting 10, 18
disappointments 24
disruptive behaviour 7, 16–17
drama therapy 49
dreams 9

drug misuse 18, 21
drug therapy 47–48
earlier experiences 28–29
eating disorders 9–10, 17
ECT 48
educational psychologists 36
electroconvulsive therapy 48
energy, lack of 9, 15
epilepsy 29
ethnic factors in depression 21
false ideas 15
family consultation centre 36, 39–49
family doctor 35–36
family therapy 41–43
friends, loss of 23–24
genes 26–28
girls, incidence of depression 19–21
group therapy 46–47
Hall, Sir Peter 2–3
hallucinations 15
headache 8

hearing voices 15
helping the depressed child 31–38
hope 33
hopelessness 12
hormones 28
hypnosis 49
hypomania 15
imipramine 48
incidence of depression 19–21
    changes over time 21
inheritance of tendency to depression 26–28
learning difficulties 29
listening 31–33
lithium carbonate 48
long-term outlook 50
loss 14–15, 23–24
ME 15
medication 47–48
mood
    sad or unhappy 7–8
    swings 15, 48
music therapy 49
myalgic encephalomyelitis 15
neurotransmitters 27
parents, action sheet for 37
personality 28
physical contact 34
physical illness
    chronic 29
    as trigger 25

physical treatments 47–48
Plath, Sylvia 3
play 12, 33
postviral fatigue syndrome 15
poverty 21
practical help 33–34
professional help 35–36
protective factors 29–30
psychiatrists 39, 40
psychologists 39–40
psychotherapists 39, 40
psychotherapy 43–45
psychotic depression 15
referral 36
role play 46
sad mood 7–8
self-blame 13
self-esteem, loss of 13
serotonin uptake inhibitors 48
sexual abuse 25, 28, 34
siblings 26
signs of depression 7–18
sisters 26
sleep disturbance 9
sleep-talking 9
sleepwalking 9
social workers 39
stomach-ache 8
stress 25
substance abuse 18, 21

suicide
    ideas of or attempts 10–13, 15, 19–20
    incidence 19
support 34
teachers
    action sheet for 38
    physical contact with pupils 34
temperament 28
tiredness 9
    persistent 15
treatment 41–49
tricyclic antidepressants 47–48
triggers of depression 22–30
unhappy mood 7–8
unipolar disorder 15
vulnerability to depression 26–29
worrying 16
young people's clinic 36, 39–49